NoDev

NoOps

NoIT

Principles governing the ideology, methodology and praxeology of informed IT decision making.

Hussein Badakhchani

Paperback edition version 1.0 August 8th 2017

2

Preface

Humour is the highest expression of human intelligence - @3laz3r

The first PC that I used was my father's Zenith 286 IBM clone. However, the first computer that I owned was a ZX Spectrum 16K which was bought as a birthday present for my older brother, and from whom I managed to appropriate in the settlement of a debt within a year of the anniversary. This transaction took place when I was around eight years old, so I can argue with some credibility that I have a lifetime's experience of both computing and finance. As a career technologist beginning in an e-commerce start-up, during the death throes of the dot com bubble, and working my way through to a tier one global investment bank, I have had the chance to distil from the many lessons learned over 20 years of experience, some key principles that have informed my IT decision making.

To make these principles and the assertions they council easier to remember and communicate, I have given them memorable, and perhaps in some cases, contentious names; hence the title of this book. My hope is that by naming these principles it will encourage general discourse and more specifically a thorough critique that will ultimately help to refine and elaborate the ideas they convey in the service IT decision makers at large. I should add that the names are probably not original, for instance the word NoOps has been used in IT since at least 2005[1]. However, in this book I have tried to give these words concise meaning in the context of informed IT decision making.

Imprecision, confusion and religiosity are sadly, the hallmarks of many discussions and debates. In a sincere attempt to address these imperfections in myself, I will define my terms with as much precision and clarity as I can, while knowing that in the final analysis they will be found wanting. The definitions that I use are a product of research, inquiry, inquisition and adversarial debate with the broader community. I hope the reader recognises that they are being presented with battled hardened and seasoned arguments. I fully expect, and look forward to, the barrage of abuse from broader IT community, not least from those who reflexively strike out at ideas that challenge the positions that they have spent much of their professional lives cultivating. I firmly believe ideas have no rights and should be subject to the cruellest tortures which the human mind is capable of imagining. However, I also believe that people have rights and must be treated with a commensurate degree of civility and humility that they demonstrate to others in line with the principle of reciprocity. Given this expectation it would be remiss of me not to initiate a pre-emptive strike against ideas and behaviours that I consider to be demonstrably pathological.

The simplification, standardisation and automation of IT; the commoditization of IT, is a long and maturing trend that is accelerating. Those that stand in front of this tsunami will be swept away as has happened in past waves of technological disruption. History is replete with examples of those unfortunates who either could not or chose not to adapt to the changing technological landscape. It is hard not to feel some sympathy for the historical casualties that have ignored the titanic spectres of Prometheus and Atlas[2], but we should have far less sympathy for the modern day equivalent of the Luddites.

The opportunities created by modern societies that have at their core a respect for the rights of life, liberty and property and a keen understanding of the balance between the role of the state and market have never been greater in human history. Those that choose not to recognise that the only certainty is uncertainty; that technological progress has an exponential trajectory and the wealth of freedoms created by these circumstances; are ultimately responsible for their own fate. I hope that this book helps to inform IT decision makers so as to ensure they are not swept away by technological progress, but also to learn to recognise and harness the potential of technology to generate value for themselves and the communities that they associate with and serve.

I stress to the reader that the guiding principles advocated in this book are just that, principles i.e. propositions that serve to inform decision making. They will serve one well, in the overwhelming majority of cases, to arrive at an informed decision *quickly*. They are not however laws to be obeyed without thought or reason, they are not universal principles, laws of physics or mathematics but they are "good enough" pragmatic and practical truths occupying a space spanning instinct, intuition, experience, wisdom and intellect.

These principles also make up the ideological constituent of Trivector Transformation. Trivector Transformation is a topic for another book, suffice to say that it is a paradigm for Digital Transformation which is distinguished by its three constituent parts: an ideology which is comprised of a core set of guiding principles; methodology which applies those principles to the domain of digital transformation; and a praxeology of actionable techniques for the management of people and technology with the express purpose of increasing an organisation's productivity by raising the capability of and capacity for human action.

For the purposes of understanding this book one can substitute ideas, methods and practices for ideology, methodology and praxeology. While there is no shortage of generally applicable and proven ideas and methods in IT decision making, guidance on practice has been far more specific in scope and limited in efficacy. The actionable practices which I advocate in this book have been in the context digital transformation of global institutions with large legacy IT estates. These are arguably the most difficult domains to affect change in IT. While the focus of this book is on the ideological principles of Trivector Transformation, it will do more than just introduce the reader to methodological and praxeological vectors of the Trivector. However, it cannot and will not be a full and exhaustive discussion on the subject.

To fully understand the perspective that these principles illuminate and the context in which they were forged I believe we have to redefine a word that we are all familiar with and which is, for me, at the centre of IT. This word is the 'computer'. It is my conviction that redefining the word in the context of enterprise IT decision making will better equip decision makers to arrive at more informed decisions for the businesses they serve. Therefore the first, second and third chapter of this book redefine the computer, define the scope of IT decision making and set the current context in which those decisions are taken. Subsequent chapters are dedicated to the principles and the assertions they make. The final chapters of the book identify praxeological actions for decision to execute. For the readers convenience the principles and assertions are listed in the contents.

The remaining chapters will describe how these principles are manifested when combined with appropriate methodology and praxeology. I can't stress the importance of bringing all three vectors (ideology, methodology and praxeology) together if one's aim is to realise the maximum possible value from the knowledge and experience captured in this book. The invocation of praxeology is a conscious acknowledgement of the teachings of the Austrian School of economics. IT decision making is informed in no small measure by an understanding of economics and I while a discussion of Austrian economics is well beyond the scope of this book I will refer the reader to essential texts.

Redefining the Computer

When I consider what people generally want in calculating, I found that it always is a number - Al-Khwarizmi

Words are tools that we use to communicate ideas, perceptions, emotions and our perspective of reality. To maximise the utility of these tools we try to agree definitions that are precise, unambiguous and which are imbued with information and meaning and ultimately their utility is weighed against the truth they convey. The various definitions of the word 'computer' offered up by the Oxford English Dictionary (OED), while technically reasonable, do little to inform contemporary decision making in IT. Let's start with definitions provided online:

"An electronic device which is capable of receiving information (data) in a particular form and of performing a sequence of operations in accordance with a predetermined but variable set of procedural instructions (program) to produce a result in the form of information or signals."

"A person who makes calculations, especially with a calculating machine."

While the former is a perfectly reasonable definition of a computer the latter is somewhat antiquated. Other definitions include: "*A device or machine performing or facilitating calculation*". The 1915 Chamber's Jrnl. July 478/1 states "*By means of this computer the task is performed mechanically and almost instantaneously.*" While we can argue the technical merits of these definitions, as someone who has spent a life time working with computers, I find they offer little utility in informing my use of computers, specifically because there is no explicit mention of automation, which I consider to be fundamental to the nature of computers.

The word *automatically* is used in only one citation for the OED definition and that is from 1941 Nature 14 June 753/2 which states:

"The telescope drive is of an elaborate nature; the effects of changing refraction, of differential flexure and of errors in the gears are automatically allowed for by a system of 'computers"

Of the many citations given for the different definitions of the word computer the word *automation* only appears in five of them, and in none of the definitions. To fail to explicitly point out that computers automate calculation is to overlook the quintessential nature of these machines and perhaps explains why we still see so much needless manual intervention in their use today. We would do well remember a quote from one of the fathers of computing, Charles Babbage:

"The economy of human time is the next advantage of machinery in manufactures"

The automation of calculation is the advantage that computers offer to humanity. I therefore suggest the following definition of a computer to better inform our understanding their utility:

"Noun: Any device or machine (physical or virtual), that increases productivity by automating cognitive and algorithmic processes"

I use 'algorithmic processes' in this definition as it encompasses the meanings of 'sequence of operations' and 'calculation'. It is important to stress the utility of computers is in most part derived from their capacity for automation, and subsequent increase in productivity that automation generates. Finally the advances of artificial intelligence and machine learning demand to be represented in the definition of the computer if we are to fully inform ourselves of the scope that these devices are capable of automating i.e. cognitive processes.

Whenever we witness repetitive manual use of computers we must recognise that the device is not being used in an optimal fashion. In fact we should consider this as a form of misuse, if not abuse, of computers. I am as guilty as anyone else in abusing computers in this way however, I am happy to report that with concerted effort to cease manual intervention and repetition when I use computers I have reduced both the frequency and duration of such abuse.

There are many reasons for failing to implement full automation. These range from: a lack of expertise; a perception that the cost of automation outweighs the benefits; a misconception that it is somehow acceptable, or part of the job description, to sit at a keyboard and repeat the same tasks day after day[3]; or to inject manual intervention into an otherwise automated process. It is an unfortunate reality, but no surprise, that such misconceptions are more prominent in the state sector. If you have to carry out a manual task using computer more than three times, you should seriously consider automating that task.

Economics of IT Decision Making

Man himself is the beginning and the end of every economy - Carl Menger

Before we can discuss the principles that govern informed IT decision making we must clarify the kind of decisions we are referring to. We need to understand the scope of IT decision making and what underpins it. Broadly speaking IT decision makers have to deal with the following classes of decisions:

- Organisational Culture & Structure – Teams, roles and responsibilities.
- Technology Strategy – Long term plans to deliver business objectives.
- Technology Stack – How to identify and select which technologies to use.
- Technology Partners – From whom to procure technology products and services.
- Financial – Controlling the costs of technology and maximising the value that it can generate.

IT decision makers face the same fundamental economic realities that are common to all branches of the business i.e. identifying the most efficient means of allocating finite resources, with the goal of realising business objectives. A working understanding of economics is critical if we are to inform IT decision making, and thus the school of economics that one subscribes to will have a huge influence, for better or worse, on the quality of decision making.

My own research, experience and observations have drawn me towards the Austrian School of economics and the works of its historical and contemporary scholars. The insights of Carl Menger, Eugen von Bohm-Bawerk and Ludwig von Mises; specifically Marginal Utility, Subjective Theory of Value and Praxeology not only provide the tools to critically analyse the options presented to decision makers but crucially, they illuminate the path to action.

Murray Rothbard's Man, Economy and State with its inclusion and elaboration of the role of entrepreneurship in production is also essential reading for those IT decision makers working in start-up firms or those seeking to create a culture of intrapreneurship in larger organisations. I strongly recommend to anyone that is responsible for making IT decision making to become familiar with the fundamental ideas of the Austrian School. Contemporary scholars whose work is readily available at the

Mises Institute or their own online channels include Dr. Joe Salerno, Robert Murphy, Thomas Woods, David Gordon, Hans-Hermann Hoppe and for some of the most perceptive and provocative analysis of economics I refer the reader to the fellow traveller Thomas Sowell.

The principles of NoDev, NoOps, NoIT and the assertions that they make are directly applicable to all of the decision classes identified above to a greater or lesser degree. I hope to demonstrate this in the following chapters.

Everything as a Service & Software Defined Everything

Boundless Computing, Unbounded IT

As I stated earlier I do not have a monopoly on the words NoDev, NoOps and NoIT and there is, unsurprisingly, the usual conflict within the IT crowd as to the definition of these words. NoOps is currently the most contentious term, loved and loathed in equal measures but I'm sure NoDev and NoIT will also have their day in the arena. The definitions I use for these words have one objective and that is to inform decision making by conveying assertions precisely and unambiguously. In an effort to achieve this objective I will describe the overarching trends in IT and nest the definitions within that context.

The most dynamic concepts in enterprise IT today are Everything as a Service and Software Defined Everything. For the purpose of this book I consider Everything As A Service (EaaS or XaaS) to not only encompass the various on demand delivery service classes: Software (SaaS), Infrastructure (IaaS) and Platform (PaaS) but also any function within the enterprise for which a demand exists to consume that service via an API (most probably a secured RESTful API).

Firstly let's be clear as to why XaaS is such a compelling proposition. IT that is delivered as a service is really an expression of the commoditization of IT. In a famous (or infamous) article published in 2003 by the Harvard Business Review, Nicholas Carr[4] drew parallels between the commoditization of IT and other technological innovations in industry such as electricity and rail roads. Over time these proprietary technologies become ubiquitous through standardisation and competition, driven in the market by entrepreneurs responding to customer demand.

Going further back in time John McCarthy speaking at the MIT Centennial in 1961 famously said:

> *"If computers of the kind I have advocated become the computers of the future, then computing may someday be organized as a public utility just as the telephone system is a public utility... The computer utility could become the basis of a new and important industry."*

When we commoditize a product or service we make it easy to obtain and consume and ultimately we can choose between different providers for the same product or service. Commoditization standardises the product or service by simplifying and automating the provisioning process. This increases the supply of the commodity and thus reduces its cost to the consumer. For anyone within the enterprise that is responsible for delivering IT, XaaS represents the most cost efficient approach for large scale and sustainable IT delivery.

The success of any IT department is ultimately a measure of the value it generates for the business in which it operates. Provisioning IT on demand at the most cost efficient price point, against agreed service levels, is at the core of running a value generating IT department. Adopting XaaS as an IT strategy fosters the simplification, standardisation and automation that is necessary to commoditize IT. In summary the enterprise should embrace XaaS to:

- Reduce or eliminate capital expenditure on technology.
- Create a more predictable operational expenditure.
- Offload the burden of regulatory and audit compliance to third party providers that specialise in meeting those requirements.
- Easily scale IT (up or down) to meet fluctuating demand.
- Rapidly respond to customer demands for new products and services.
- Reallocate resources from the cost of doing business (IT) to generating revenue (the business).

Beyond the three demand delivery service classes (SaaS, IaaS and PaaS) there are a range of fundamental IT services that span the enterprise that include:

Logging as a Service (LaaS) - All applications generate logs however, until recently IT departments have been slow to realise the huge benefits of centrally managing these logs and offering consolidated views of logs from multiple, distributed application components. On a personal note I think a simple measure of the effectiveness of IT can be measured by how quickly an engineer can access the information they need to support a distributed system. If it takes more and a few seconds then I simply don't rate your system however good you think it is. I know it costs too much to support and it is too unresponsive.

Monitoring as a Service (MaaS) - Variance in the type, quality and temporal availability (real time or historical) of metrics across applications within the enterprise is another highly significant source of inefficiency.

Security as a Service (SECaaS) - Providing a standard set of authentication, authorisation, attribution and encryption services that can be consumed by all applications in the enterprise is a vast improvement in terms of quality and costs over maintaining disparate security solutions.

Regulation, Audit and Compliance as a Service (RACaaS) - Giving regulators, auditors and compliance teams the services they need to perform their routine tasks is an imperative for any business operating in heavily regulated sectors and jurisdictions. The cost of these activities, mostly ad-hoc and manual in nature, and the disruption they cause to the enterprise should not be underestimated.

The above are just a few examples of IT activities that can, at least to some extent, be delivered as enterprise services. The growth in XaaS is explosive and not restricted to technology services, indeed there are organisations now that are beginning to question the need for large numbers of fixed managers and executives in IT which are experimenting with Management as a Service. The concept is novel in that it returns management to a facilitation role rather than a leadership role; an approach which I believe has considerable merit[5].

Now that we have established the 'why' and 'what' to deliver as XaaS, let's consider the 'how' and this is where the notion of Software Defined Everything plays a significant role in informing our decisions.

There is much hype attached to Software Defined Everything and arguably little of substance. This is an area that demands the attention of IT decision makers. If we are to follow the assertions of NoDev, NoOps and NoIT it should be of no surprise that we find they lead us away from hardware and appliance based solutions towards software and services. By configuring our IT infrastructure in software it becomes easily accessible via APIs and there we:

- Maximise disintermediation in our operating model and create lean, highly efficient and specialised teams. Such teams can support their services far more effectively than teams whose specialisations are delineated across technology boundaries and who have no special interest in the services deployed to the infrastructure.
- Encourage automation by exposing standardised API's that any application owner can choose to consume to automate common, repetitive tasks.
- Reduce the time and effort required to affect configuration changes.

It is my contention that the war between application teams and infrastructure teams (application development vs middleware, database, storage and networks) that has been raging since the inception of Enterprise IT is now over. The application teams won. I will describe how and why the victory was achieved when we delve into the NoOps principle, suffice to say within IT engineering, we are all developers. Some of us develop applications and some of develop infrastructures but both roles now utilise as their primary mode of working software code. We should also note that some individuals can occupy both roles seamlessly, these are Full Stack Developers that have arisen in significant numbers during the last decade and some of those are now morphing into Full Spectrum Technologists. Such individuals are, in my opinion the most valuable IT resources one can find.

As I've already alluded to above I firmly believe that the commoditization of IT is in large part the direct result of market dynamics, that is, entrepreneurs taking risks to predict future customer demands for technology. The grandeur of the market should not be lost on those of us that are responsible for meeting the demands of IT consumers within and external to the enterprise however, rather than attempting to take on the role of the entrepreneur I would suggest that instead we endeavour to create markets for IT services within the enterprise.

As IT decision makers we have it in our power to build platforms upon which application teams can deploy their services, whatever they may be. We can't and shouldn't try to imagine what they will deploy nor which services will be demanded by their customers and which ones will fail. Beyond providing a range of fundamental services that maximise the number of market participants (adoption of our platform) and the efficiency and security of their operations, we would do well to let the market decide what is innovative and successful while we focus on enhancing the market itself.

The only way that has ever been discovered to have a lot of people cooperate together voluntarily is through the free market. And that's why it's so essential to preserving individual freedom. – Milton Friedman

NoDev

Developers are your most valuable assets, deploy them wisely - @DigiSelfDef

The principle of NoDev primarily concerns itself with the Technology Strategy, Technology Stack and Technology Partner classes of IT decision making. As with all the principles that we will discuss in this book, it will have some influence in the other decision classes.

The first assertion of the NoDev principle is:

If you are not in the business of IT, stop making IT your business

It's funny how many business have started to publically identify themselves as technology firms, but what isn't very funny (at least for the stakeholders of those businesses) is the inevitably high failure rate of the technology projects they pursue, and capital they misallocate when they start to compete with real IT businesses. Let's be clear about what an IT business is. If your primary source of revenue is derived from the sale of hardware, software and services created by your business, then you are in the business of IT. If your main sources of revenue are derived from services that consume IT, which is sourced primarily from third parties then, you are not in the business of IT.

The reasons why it is important to understand which sector of the economy your business operates within are manifold and should be obvious to anyone that has even a cursory understanding of market fundamentals. I won't spend time elaborating the reasons here beyond noting that identifying customers, competitors, employees, opportunities, threats and planning for all of these factors is predicated largely on knowing what markets your business operates within. Glibly rebranding your business as a technology business is a very risky business, so why are so many organisations jumping on this bandwagon?

There are at least two reasons why organisations and people like to believe (and want others to also believe) they are in the business of IT. The first of these should be obvious to anyone that has worked in the financial sector, however I have to admit it wasn't obvious to me until a discussion I had with the head of HR of a fast growing global payments organisation. When I explained to her the first assertion of NoDev and naively suggested they are in the payments processing business (by the way the clue is in the name of the company) she was quick refute my suggestion and insisted they were in the IT business. When I asked her who they believed were their main competitors in that sector she reeled off the names of well-established payment processors and a few FinTech start-ups. As she did so in a moment of honestly and clarity she added, "Ah, I think I see what you mean, but we'll never raise any capital if we go to investors and tell them we're a Bank!"

Rebranding an organisation to benefit from capital flows or to reduce the perceived damage of being associated with a sector that is suffering financially, may or may not, be a sensible tactical decision. The danger is that you'll start to believe your own BS and start making some pretty bad decisions. I have to say from my own experience it is highly probable that the organisation as a whole will start to believe the BS. If you really believe redefining your organisation to benefit from or reduce the risk of being associated with one sector or another, do so with extreme caution.

The second reason for wanting to believe that one works for a technology firm is a mix of inferiority complex while at the same time attempting to increase pay or mimic the working conditions of technology firms. The best practices and the working cultures of technology firms are making their way into in other sectors. However, these superficial environmental changes do not justify believing that you work for a Silicon Valley start-up. As for the inferiority complex that some technologists suffer from, which drives from the need to believe they work for a technology company, when in fact, they work in an IT department of a financial institution; all I can suggest is to not allow the pathology to spread. These individuals are probably unnecessarily resentful at their lot and should probably be encouraged to seek work in other organisations[6].

The second assertion of the NoDev principle is:

Only commit development resources and engage with projects which demonstrably, unambiguously and unequivocally generate revenue for the business or enhance customer experience

This may be a difficult message for many IT decision makers to hear, including those in the financial sector with mature IT divisions. But history is on my side, and the trend is inextricable. Many aspects of IT are fast becoming commodities or being delivered and consumed as utilities as I have described earlier.

Acting in recognition of this long and maturing trend, it is incumbent upon IT decision makers to exercise far greater control in the approval of any project that demands internal development effort. To help identify development projects to which enterprise resources should not be allocated, NoDev asserts avoiding development effort in any non-core or ancillary system, or developing any product for which existing mature third-party products already exist.

In my time, I've seen IT departments recreate all manner of existing applications: databases, enterprise service buses, continuous build and delivery tools, and all under the false pretence that there was no software available that could deliver exactly what was required. If the decision makers in these instances were enforcing the NoDev principle such projects would never have seen the light of day, saving a huge amount of time, money and embarrassment.

Before jumping into coding a solution the business needs to make sure IT has evaluated, in order of priority:

- Community Software (business friendly versions of Free and Open Source Software).
- Proprietary Software.
- Open Source APIs and libraries.
- Proprietary APIs and libraries.
- The last option should be the allocation of valuable development resources.

Such evaluations need not take months to compete. Typically only a handful of vendors meet the basic criteria and the shortlisted vendors can present their case and be evaluated in a matter of weeks.

The third assertion of DevOps principle is:

It's not a matter of Build vs Buy; it's political, technical and economical

Build vs buy, has historically been one of the most common and most contentious questions that arise in Enterprise IT. Every aspect of this question, including the question itself has come under critique from different camps. In one of my favourite rants Coverlet Meshing tells us that 'Build Vs. Buy is a Dangerous Lie'. Coverlet asserts that both "Build" and "Buy" are ultimately integration efforts but that "Buy" decisions indicate disinvestment and a move toward Commodity IT accompanied with "an exodus of ambitious hackers, ever-vigilant about remaining relevant...leaving behind non-technical project managers (the overzealous and process-focused) and technical order-takers (under-motivated second- and third-tier engineers)".

This is a compelling argument and I cannot deny that I have directly observed this phenomenon and have read dozens of case studies that at least in part can be explained by Coverlet's assertions.

Coverlet refers to buying off-the-shelf software but I will assume he includes all Commodity IT (SaaS, PaaS and IaaS) in his argument and ultimately finishes off his case by rescinding the lie: "The honesty of it is that if your business model (and talent) can't manage a build, then you won't be able to deliver a buy."

It is worth mentioning that Coverlet describes himself as "picking a fight with anyone who doesn't understand that banks are actually software companies and need to invest in engineering as a core competency". As a proponent of the NoDev principle I believe that while banks are in the business of providing financial services to their customers with a clearly stated goal of generating a profit for their shareholders and other stakeholders, they are certainly not software companies.

For now I want to emphasise an insight of Coverlet's that I share, which is the impact of Digital Transformation on in-house talent. The reality is that if one cannot get the buy-in of the most talented technologist and engineers in the enterprise, your efforts in will probably fail, in precisely the manner described by Coverlet.

On the other hand insisting on building everything and pretending all your IT staff are esteemed savants is also a doomed strategy. These are the transformation failures you will never hear about; drowned out by the sound of thunderous back slapping[7] and the hushed whispers of geniuses employed in "extreme performance disciplines" where artisans are hard at work manually crafting the next expensive failure.

The reality is that every build vs buy decision has a political dimension which cannot be avoided and which can be significantly different from one business to the next and as such we cannot draw any general inferences that will help to inform our decision making without including that political dimension alongside the economic and technological dimensions.

If introducing new third party technology will result in losing talent from your business, then you must recognise and understand the risks and costs associated with that decision, and attempt to mitigate them accordingly. There will be instances where you will have no choice but to manage out some very good people that are simply not going to reskill or adopt new roles to help them adapt to the new technology landscape. This is often an unavoidable part of introducing new technology. That said there is much that can be done to avoid the loss of talent as a result of new technology and there is plenty of management and HR literature to help you maintain your staff. My suggestion is to read it.

NoOps

In the City respect is everything – Grand Theft Auto

The principle of NoOps is primarily concerned with the Organisational Culture and Structure and Financial classes of decision making. Given its long use in IT and the relatively recent mainstream adoption of DevOps, Cloud Infrastructure, XaaS and Software Defined Everything, NoOps demands some context before I proceed to define it.

NoOps is NOT getting rid of IT Operations

One of the most common and enduring uses of the word NoOps is to refer to eliminating IT operations entirely. The problem with such definitions is that they conveniently scope IT operations in a manner that allows them to be eliminated with a seemingly shiny nugget of technology. Such definitions of NoOps do nothing to inform IT decision makers; in fact they are more likely to simply embarrass anyone that seriously subscribes to them. All that is required to defeat the notion of eliminating operations is to take an honest look at the full scope of work carried out by a productive operations team.

IT operations roles are not static in the face of changing technology; they evolve, arguably more rapidly than application roles. The original activities of racking, stacking, cabling and administering IT infrastructures in a typical enterprise has been hugely diminished by outsourcing, commoditization and the advent of cloud infrastructure, however new activities in software development life cycle, automated provisioning, monitoring, metering and security now engender demands that are difficult to satisfy by employment markets. NoOps is not about eliminating operations; rather it is concerned with maximising productivity in IT operations.

NoOps advocates the elimination of human intervention in IT operations through the use of technology and automation. By operations we not only mean the teams that traditionally support production infrastructures, but all operations with IT systems, so for example many forms of testing, build processes, security and vulnerability patching would all be included in the scope of operations. I also refer to operations teams as infrastructure teams interchangeably. This is a direct result of speed at which operations roles are evolving and blurring traditional boundaries.

Some of the key reasons why automation is desirable over manual intervention include:

- Speed - humans executing repetitive cognitive and algorithmic processes pertaining to the management of IT infrastructure are going to be undeniably and drastically slower than computers.
- Error Prone - it doesn't matter how many times a human has executed a repetitive function, statistically they will make errors far more frequently than computers.
- Costly - Whenever one assigns a human to do work that a computer can carry out, you can expect a substantial rise in the total cost of that activity to your business.
- Insecure - Humans can be easily manipulated to leak data, open access or otherwise compromise the security of your business.

I strongly recommend readers visit Adrian Cockcroft's Blog: "Ops, DevOps and PaaS (NoOps) at Netflix"[8]. Here's a short quote from that entry to whet your appetite:

This is part of what we call NoOps. The developers used to spend hours a week in meetings with Ops discussing what they needed, figuring out capacity forecasts and writing tickets to request changes for the datacentre. Now they spend seconds doing it themselves in the cloud.

All the activities described above, the information exchange between developers and operations, capacity forecasts, change requests, etc. are needless dependencies created between developers and operations that once removed naturally allow the simplification of processes, their standardization and ultimately their automation.

This first assertion of NoOps principle is:

Eliminate all dependencies between application developers and infrastructure developers

Deploying code into any environment should be the job of the application team that owns the code, **not the infrastructure team that owns the infrastructure**.

By making centralized operations teams responsible for execution of code releases to infrastructure that they "own" is, in my opinion, an appalling misallocation of enterprise resources. This form of organisation makes the infrastructure team accountable for something they know nothing about (the application) and disenfranchises the development team forcing them to "knowledge transfer" to the operations team when they should be coding the next set of features demanded by your customers.

What is more, one almost invariably finds that the centralized operations team seem to take pride in the extent of manual intervention captured in their runbook. The amount of manual poking of systems is almost a measure of their importance and a reflection of their job security.

Rather than allocating resources to building the systems that facilitate fully automated provisioning (build, test, deploy and destroy) time is wasted dealing with lengthy release cycles and mopping up the misconfigurations after every deployment.

Application teams should have the ability, given the correct roles and access controls, to self-service their infrastructure. To deploy their code, make any necessary configuration changes and liaise with other stakeholders' without any intervention from operations and in a manner that is fully traceable to auditors. This can be facilitated, safely, on shared infrastructure given the use of the appropriate container technologies that can isolate workloads and user APIs that lift the burdens of regulatory and compliance demands on process workflow.

Just as every line of code should be considered a liability and not an asset, every manual intervention should be considered a misallocation of resource in poorly thought out process which is costing your business, alienating your employees and destroying creativity and value.

There are multiple strategies for eliminating silos and dependencies between application and infrastructure teams but the most powerful approach I have utilised has to been to use off premise cloud technology and to include infrastructure developers within the application team. Infrastructure developers are part and parcel of the application team. They are embedded with application developers, attend daily stand-ups and play a critical role in the continuous delivery of the application. The use of off premise cloud infrastructure essentially means the infrastructure developers are responsible for defining operations and infrastructure architecture in software.

The second assertion of the NoOps principle is:

Eliminate all human intervention in IT operations

While we may never be able to fully automate every aspect of our operations, for example some regulators demand four eyes process approval and execution; we must rigorously challenge the unthinking orthodoxy which currently governs many IT processes. Automate, simplify and standardise; I subscribe to this mantra but one has to proceed in the right order, that is, simplify, standardise and then automate otherwise you literally risk making an ASS out of your IT automation efforts.

I can say with a high degree of certainty that any failure to automate a process could probably be traced back having made no attempt to simplify the process before automating it. No attempt was made to challenge the process; to question who is doing what and why before automating it. Indeed no effort was made to question the existence of the process in the first instance.

Once a process has been simplified, standardizing it follows almost naturally. Stakeholders adopt your process because is it simple, it saves them time and generates value for them.

The opposite is also true; a poorly thought-out, complex process will never win buy-in from users. Any attempt to put lipstick on such a pig will be fraught with difficulty and often resulting in the vast majority of users and stakeholders finding exceptions to your attempts to increase adoption of the offending process.

Simplified, standardized process with broad adoption, are the ideal targets for automation. They yield the largest benefit in terms of productivity gains per unit cost and also have the benefit of increasing stakeholders' confidence in IT with every process that is successfully automated. Once a culture of automation has been created a virtuous spiral of simplification, standardization and automation is established resulting in continuous improvement. A culture of automation will also attract the right kind of talent to the business, i.e. knowledge workers that want to generate value for their co-workers and customers, not IT workers that want to plumb hardware into datacentres; infrastructure and operations developers not button pushers.

Ultimately NoOps is simply the most optimal way to design and implement IT operations given the constraint to maximize productivity, while securing the business. The alternative is a misallocation of resources, and the managers making those decisions should, I am afraid, be swiftly removed for the sake of the investors in that business.

NoIT

Time, unstitched from the fabric of space by enquiring minds, spun into mortal coils without design

As a career technologist I haven't suddenly given up my enthusiasm for technology and turned into a Luddite, despite having witnessed some misguided uses of technology and computers.

The NoIT principle concerns itself with the Financial and Strategic classes of decision making. The first assertion of the NoIT principle is:

Eliminate IT systems that demand the attention of humans

To put it another way, when you decide to introduce that shiny new risk tracker, architecture taxonomy repository, knowledge management system, document management system, procurement system, etc. if the intent is to expose these systems to others to populate with data and use, then it has to be the responsibility of the team that is introducing this system to ensure the highest standards of user experience. The highest standard of user experience for any administrative function is that the user **doesn't** experience it at all.

Systems that demand end users to acquire the expertise to use them in order to fulfil a demand which is not directly related to the most productive aspects of their role are essentially misallocating resources en-masse. As more of these IT systems creep into the organisation you'll notice the following change to the talent composition within the organisation. Those individuals that can either totally avoid the demands being made by these systems or those that master the management of non-essential IT, prosper.

Your organisation acquires a wealth of process savvy employees whether or not that was the intention. Either they can raise a PO, request various services, fill out vendor management questionnaires with their eyes closed or they can convince someone else to do it for them. In the meantime your attrition rate soars to new heights, technology stagnates and innovation becomes a costly exercise hiring and firing new "innovation" teams.

There may be justifiable reasons for having such systems but if there is, then the teams that own them must be held accountable for ensuring they place a minimal burden on other employees. For example, I have worked in places where as a technologist I barely noticed that I was placing a purchase order, liaising directly with data centre staff, filling out vendor on-boarding requests etc. But I've also worked in places where as a technologist it has felt like such operations have taken months to complete; dealing with both IT systems and people that simply didn't work.

The difference between these experiences is a function of how IT is perceived and used by the organisation, i.e. is customer centricity and user experience held in high regard? Where the experience was painless there were invariably people that would volunteer to do the administration for me, mostly from the very team that owned the system, but on some occasions it would be other people that considered offering support to be of little cost to them. Where the experience was a nightmare, the system owners would only tell me about the system and process in great detail (information that I really did not want nor need to know). They would be quick to tell me why they, and I, were forced to use the system and they would even extol the many benefits of the system. They never, ever, offered to do the administration for me. That is the tell-tale sign of costly and poorly designed IT.

Let me be clear, I am an advocate of self-service but only for services that improve my productivity, not functions that are required to satisfy the administration of the business. The distinction I draw between a service and a function is simple; services generate revenue, improve productivity and create value. Functions pertain to process efficiency for administrative, bureaucratic, audit, compliance and regulatory demands. Well-designed functions can save time and money, but they never generate revenue.

The second assertion of the NoIT principle is:

Use IT to expose services to customers and employees not administrative functions owned by specialists

It is easy to spot when a function is being exposed to employees in the guise of a service. When you attempt to use the "service" you end up learning a huge amount about the underlying process from all the various people that you have to liaise with in order to guide you through the system. In effect, all the IT is doing is shielding the team responsible for the function from doing their work. Instead it is offloading the work to unsuspecting employees that have ended up straying into an administrative malaise.

It is not uncommon to find these administrative teams staffed by an army of contractors that have no empathy for the employees that get caught up in their systems. Indeed the longer it takes to get the job done, the more people that are involved and the more complex the process is, the better it is for them, for obvious financial reasons.

It should be noted that such teams are an extremely attractive target for optimisation and transformation within the enterprise. Not only will you reduce costs significantly by reforming them, but the unintended consequences are extremely positive for employees, customers and investors alike.

The third assertion of NoIT principle is:

Eliminate IT duplication across the enterprise

A sustained absurdity is a key indicator of corruption - @DigiSelfDef

It's bad enough to have to deal with a myriad of administrative IT systems that demand human attention, but the problem is compounded by duplicate and competing systems owned by different divisions. Sometimes the duplication is in IT services as well, for example having two "Enterprise Standard" services buses.

IT decision makers must pick one service; create a migration plan to cover any barriers to adoption of that service, which should include resourcing to fill functional gaps and notifying customers of the improvements they can expect. Set a date to decommission the duplicate service and finally ensure that the duplicate service is decommissioned. This is not rocket science. It simply requires leadership and the will to execute the decision. If migration fails, the first people that should be relieved of their duties are the management of the duplicate service[9]. Then rinse and repeat.

Whether the enterprise is embarking upon transformation, consolidating after a merger and acquisition, or simply attempting to reduce costs or eliminating duplicate IT systems and services, one of the key goals is to always drive efficiency in IT.

Maintaining multiple systems that perform the same or similar functions will always be more costly than maintaining a single system. Among the places to look for consolidation and efficiencies are: human resources, IT hardware and software, as well as other vendor agreements for professional services, maintenance etc.

Let's review some common sources of duplication and discuss some strategies for eliminating this type of duplication when it arises. Here are some of the key places where duplication can originate:

Mergers and acquisitions

Source: Where IT duplication is born of M&A, the acquirer typically chooses the target state with the superseding applications and services.

Strategy: Any gaps in functionality that arise out of decommissioning applications are handled by enhancing functionality within the replacement applications and services.

Internal re-organization

Source: In re-organization where managed services exist for IT, verticals are instructed to consume the managed services and decommission their IT. Duplicate IT services are found in an exercise to identify the current state across all verticals.

Strategy: The target state definition will accommodate the singular workloads. The case where managed services do not already exist demands greater attention. I address this below in the strategy for "Attempting to eliminate duplication."

Managed services

Source: If the managed services provided by IT are of poor quality, shadow IT will be considered as the only viable option by business units. Invariably the business units will not coordinate IT strategy, resulting in a menagerie of duplicate IT.

Strategy: Ensuring managed services fully cover customer use cases for workloads and SLAs is fundamental for increasing adoption of managed services. This will drive down duplication and obviate the need to pursue shadow IT.

Poor governance

Source: In large organizations with poor IT governance and control, duplicate IT systems will proliferate as a natural result of business units pursuing their strategic interests. Poor governance is a consequence of weak leadership. Duplication in IT can arise from ignorance of managed services or wilful refusal to de-dupe IT, even when managed services are clearly suitable for the use cases being implemented by the business unit.

Strategy: Simple but powerful tools for correcting these behaviours come from user communities and performance objective alignment. User communities with participation from all business units can reduce the lack of communication and awareness that can lead to the creation of duplicate IT through ignorance. You could also connect managers' bonuses (or the lack thereof) to the degree of adoption of managed services within their in business units. This can have a catalytic effect on adoption and potentially drive a cultural shift as managers that are unwilling to de-dupe eventually leave the organization.

Attempting to eliminate duplication

Source: A most unfortunate outcome of some de-duping efforts is the introduction of duplication. This situation can arise when the decision is taken to introduce a new system when upgrading an existing system or as a target state with the intent of decommissioning other applications.

Strategy: The introduction of new systems always carries a risk of duplicating existing functions, application and services and for this reason alone one should consider the alternative approach of picking an existing system for the target state and investing in that system rather than a new one.

Remember, picking existing systems may not always be an option, but in my experience this option is too readily dismissed in favour of introducing new technology from scratch. Selecting and investing in an existing system is also, on whole, a less risky proposition and one that can be return on investment more quickly, especially if duplicate systems can be decommissioned quickly.

Finally selecting a target state system from an existing portfolio can be an effective first step toward the transformation of the particular workload in question.

DevOps Methodology and PaaS Technology

Developers, developers, developers, developers, deodorant… Steve Ballmer

For the purpose of this book I consider software, systems and service development life cycle (SDLC) as broadly being the same thing; a series of steps that provide a model for the development and management of software, systems or services. Any entity engaged in the creation of one or more these S's will have an SDLC, no matter how informal it may be.

The necessity of formalising an SDLC into a process that is regulated, secure and compliant is a function of the size and nature of the business. Factors such as the jurisdictional boundaries (local, national, regional or global) in which the business operates, and the awareness of the total cost of developing and maintaining software, systems and or services also influence the SDLC. A detailed discussion of SDLC is beyond the scope of this book suffice to say, a global enterprise probably maintains more than one SDLC and has a menagerie of different applications (code and binary repositories, software registries, continuous build, test and delivery tools, etc.) often duplicating functions and duplicating SDLC processes.

If this situation isn't complex enough, throw into the mix, the traditional silos and dependencies inflicted by outmoded organisational models. For example the separation of development, testing, release management and operations, unsurprisingly results in a situation where release cycles take months.

Such environments foster attrition and your best development talent will leave to join start-ups out of frustration. Over time what remains in your talent pool will be a potent mix of individuals that either know-how to subvert the rules or worse still actively engage in their creation. These individuals make no useful contribution, and simply engage in fighting a losing battle with entropy using change requests and approval gates as their weapons of choice.

The picture painted above may be overly bleak and somewhat exaggerated but I'm sure it's a familiar picture for many experienced IT professionals. Adam Curtis's documentary series 'Pandora's Box' captures the essence of the absurdity that can arise from the implementation of what seems to be a rational plan to manage complexity and perhaps should be watched by all IT decision makers.

The unintended consequence of Enterprise SDLC is to impede the progress of code into production and with it, value generation for the business and the creation of overwhelming frustration of those creative individuals involved in producing software, systems or services.

Enter DevOps

DevOps as a culture, practice and tool set is penetrating the enterprise today because it has delivered results which are unambiguously superior to traditionally silo organised IT with all its built-in cultural in and out groups, bizarre RACI that makes operations staff accountable for applications and which lets the developers off the hook as soon as the code is in production.

Early and stunning success has left the business craving more DevOps from IT and the market has responded to the demand in what I believe is an excellent expression of innovation. In little more than a decade (we were doing DevOps before it was called DevOps) the culture, technology and the market have driven DevOps awareness, if not quite full implementation, into every sector that produces IT.

However if we step back and look at the scale of Enterprise SDLC we can see how DevOps, on its own, will not fully meet the high expectations it has raised for the enterprise. The diagram below depicts a classic Enterprise SDLC. While DevOps permeates many aspects of SDLC clearly there are gaps, most significantly in the provisioning and maintenance of the infrastructure underpinning Enterprise IT.

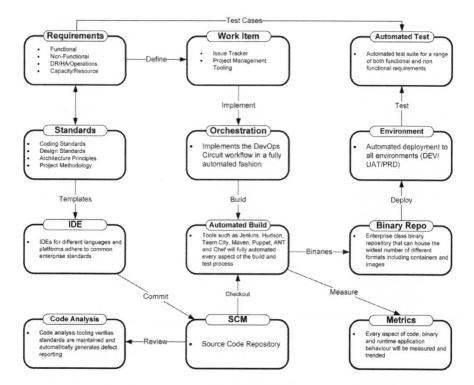

The gaps that DevOps leaves are filled using PaaS technology and the resurgence of PaaS owes much to DevOps and the recognition of the need and ability to automate not only application and infrastructure provisioning but also the IT processes demanded by Enterprise SDLC.

Defining Platform as a Service

Before we dive into the benefits of PaaS let's take a moment to define exactly what we mean by the term Platform as a Service. As with all IT terminology many different definitions exist. In choosing between them we must identify the one that best informs our purpose, so we need a definition that encapsulates the essential benefits of PaaS. For me an excellent definition comes from my colleagues at 451 Research:

PaaS is a cloud-enabled development platform that is designed to support the entire application lifecycle – including development, testing, deployment, runtime, hosting (either self-provided or by a third party) and delivery. Internal developers can optimise the creation of custom applications on PaaS and ISVs can rapidly deliver new services with PaaS

This definition precisely captures what many IT organisations within the enterprise recognise as being the key goal for the introduction of cloud based technologies, which is to optimise the productivity of their IT assets to better deliver the products and services demanded by the business.

The essence of all technology is to increase the capability and the capacity of human action. Let's see how PaaS fulfils this essence:

Self-Service, User Experience and APIs

A distinguishing feature for any PaaS is the careful implementation of self-service user experience and associated APIs. Systems that simply expose users to self-service processes without first simplifying and standardising those processes will impose heavy productivity losses to their users[10]. Furthermore, over the lifetime of a system and in an environment of continual restructuring such systems may be exposed to users for whom they were never designed. For self-service to realise expected productivity gains and cost reduction targets, the users' experience is paramount. Recently the industry has recognised that advanced IT users demand APIs to allow them to enrich and automate standardised processes to meet their specific requirements. An industry consensus has formed around the use of RESTFul Web Service APIs to fulfil this need. Where PaaS self-service capabilities have been designed and implemented well, users will naturally gravitate to their use as an alternative to using more cumbersome or manual processes.

Pre-Integrated Technology Stacks

The traditional approach of designing products around individual applications results in customers having to integrate the applications of their technology stack. While the task of integration may not be onerous it still demands manual intervention and often requires customers to manage their estate using multiple administrative channels. A key feature of the technical strategy for PaaS will be the ability to design products around workloads that satisfy business use cases rather than applications. For example one of the most common business use cases is for Online Transaction Processing (OLTP). A traditional technology stack would include Web Hosting, Application Hosting and Database Hosting products to be ordered separately and configured by the customers using potentially three different portals. A well designed PaaS will have the capability of providing a single product with pre-integrated applications (Web Server, App Server, Database) and a single portal/API for administering the underlying components.

On-Demand Provisioning

A fundamental capability of Cloud Architecture is the dynamic, on-demand resource allocation model. A singular failure of traditional upfront provisioning of compute resources is the propensity for application owners to over provision resources either to meet anticipated peak demands, or simply to obviate the need to engage in often lengthy and complex processes to obtain new infrastructure. PaaS can provide seamless auto scaling and on-demand resource provisioning which can be fully integrated with capacity management and billing systems. Beyond the expected efficiency gains in overall resource consumption there are associated gains in productivity for both application and operations teams born of more agile operations.

Automation

Automation has long been recognised as key benefit of PaaS. While the benefits of automated provisioning of infrastructure, integration with ancillary systems and simplified automated controls have long been understood, we are now seeing the integration and automation of SDLC and DevOps circuits rising to the forefront of automation efforts. The workloads that constitute continuous build, integration and delivery have corresponding products in all third party PaaS implementations and a huge amount of resources is being allocated to optimising enterprise SDLC. PaaS will be natural host for these workloads.

Catalysing Innovation

Current service delivery models do not recognise or provide the infrastructure required to facilitate innovation. The need for IT departments to offer free trial, PoC and Pilot environments has never been stronger. In many enterprises the processes that govern the provisioning of the necessary infrastructure for experimentation actively prohibit innovation. One solution to this approach, which I believe is a costly failure, is the introduction of innovation labs. Ultimately however, I believe low cost, but highly sophisticated IT infrastructure that mirrors production environments and which is located on premise is the best way to deliver the IT that incubates innovation. Teams embarking upon innovation face high costs, both temporal and financial in obtaining the, often ephemeral, infrastructure they need.

Developer Productivity

The measure of any PaaS technology is arguably the degree to which it increases developer productivity. The importance of this metric is encapsulated by an ideal to achieve 'Ideation to production multiple times a day'. In our current state even when our platforms can technically deliver this ideal, manual approval processes effectively conspire to severely limit the realisation of ideas and innovation into production. PaaS can provide the platform to allow process owners to automate checks, approvals and other artefacts of production deployment, eliminating the barriers that impede production deployment.

Infrastructure Compliance

Exposing the demands of regulatory regimes for IT infrastructure compliance to application teams results in huge productivity loss and duplication of effort. The problem is compounded when applications are deployed globally across multiple jurisdictions. A well designed PaaS effectively shields application owners not only from the burden of infrastructure compliance but also the entire process of responding to regulators demands for audit and reporting. Traditionally the cost benefit analysis of PaaS in this space has focused on cost avoidance, but given the increasingly invasive and complex demands of regulators, we are seeing a greater consideration being given to productivity as a benefit over cost avoidance.

Patching and Upgrades

The cadence of hardware and software patching is increasing as is the number of artefacts that are subject to patch management. The sheer size and complexity of IT infrastructures maintained by application owners coupled with the downtime required by infrastructure service providers for patching means that there exist today applications that simply cannot sustain patching cycles demanded by security policies. Much of the problem stems from the infrastructure providers themselves, using antiquated methods for patching or with whom our aspirations and SLAs do not align. Third party PaaS technologies now provide an array of capabilities aim at delivering 'Ever Green' infrastructure. For on premise PaaS this means fully automating all aspects of software patching and upgrades and for off-premise PaaS the whole notion of hardware patching and upgrades is obviated, becoming the concern of cloud service provider. It is also worth mentioning Runtime Application Self Protection and Virtual Patching. These technologies are changing the way we secure and patch applications in ways that force us to completely rethink traditional approaches.

Controls, Metering, Monitoring, Alerting and Reporting

All of these capabilities are now available 'natively' on third party PaaS products and are exposed for consumption either through API's or products. There are significant advantages for having these capabilities embedded in the PaaS directly rather than attempting to integrate disparate technologies such as: eliminating duplicate or very similar products, reducing integration to simple configuration and generally centralizing these functions, simplifying their overall management and consumption overhead. While we should plan to fully exploit all native capabilities in PaaS products we should also recognise that existing collateral remains extremely valuable and indeed will accelerate the development of products by obviating the need to rebuild existing capability in the 3rd Party PaaS products in the short term.

Innovative Appropriation

Good artists copy, great artists steal - Pablo Picasso

Anyone who has spent even a short period of time working in or with, the FinTech sector would have witnessed innovation project after innovation project fail and innovation teams come and go, having generated little or no value for the enterprises that funded their R&D and PoC work.

Indeed many enterprises now have well established innovation teams, with well-established records of poor performance. In an effort to increase value from innovation, enterprises are being urged to tolerate failure. "Fail Fast Fail Often" is the mantra from Silicon Valley and senior executives from enterprises are being urged to repeat the mistakes of the entrepreneurs in the IT sector.

This course of action, to take large risks on developing software to deliver services for which demand isn't clear and where competition is typically fierce, is a clear violation of the NoDev principle.

Attempting to emulate the success of IT entrepreneurs is, by definition, an incredibly risky strategy. For every IT innovation success story there are countless failures that will never see the light of day. The organisational strategies employed by the successful entrepreneurs were forged in an environment of Darwinian competition with large bets being made on the success of their efforts and fortunes being lost (or taxes being written-off) on their failures.

For an established global entity to attempt a whole sale appropriation, copying like for like the approach taken by IT firms to create their own products and services, is simply statistically doomed to fail. The question for IT decision makers is:

What is the alternative to statistically stacked failure?

To answer this question we need to examine the causes of innovation failure in the enterprise namely: failure to deliver and failure to adopt.

Failure to deliver is born of all the usual causes of project failure. Poor requirements, lack of skills, attrition, budget, etc. but most importantly of all, the one factor that acts as a force multiplier for all the other causes, the size of the project.

I simply haven't seen any large budget (say a budget of £2.5MM+) innovation project succeed. Let me be clear, I'm not saying such projects didn't advertise success; there was budget enough for that. I'm saying they never delivered anywhere near the expectations that they set and in most cases they failed to the extent that they didn't deliver at all (with the subsequent attrition of staff led by the senior managers that owned those projects). Or they disappeared into oblivion within 18 months of going live.

The second reason for failure is adoption. In this case the project actually delivers but, nobody wanted the damn innovation in the first instance. I won't elaborate this reason further beyond saying it is not enough to have senior management buy-in for the innovation; customers must demand it.

Innovate the Way You Appropriate Innovation

Rather than copying the actions of IT entrepreneurs in the hope of somehow emulating their success in the vein of B. F. Skinner's classic study of "Superstition in the Pigeon"[11] it would be far more productive to appropriate the output of the successful entrepreneurs, and in order to maintain an edge we need to select winners before they become winners.

There are now plenty of innovation incubators with a myriad of start-up organisations to choose from. In fact the whole process of engaging with and selecting a technology partner is getting easier all the time. The investment the enterprise needs to make is measured in time and intelligence not big budgets.

Leaving the selection of an innovation partner to a single team in the enterprise (it may be the innovation team if they're not busy inventing square wheels) increases the risk of missed opportunities or making a poor selection. Unless that team has a solid understanding of the market for innovation within the enterprise, they will fail to bring producers and consumers of innovation together in a successful transaction.

A better approach is for the enterprise to create and foster co-operation (as opposed to collaboration[12]) in the form of virtual appropriation teams. Such teams are ephemeral in the sense that they are not materialised in organisational hierarchies and reporting lines and will typically disperse once the project has delivered.

Appropriation teams will consist of technology suppliers, both internal and external to the enterprise and technologists that can match the suppliers' technologies to the demands of the customers within the enterprise. The internal technologists are in fact a type of entrepreneur; referred to as Enterprisers or Intrapreneurs. The innovation team, if it is to survive at all, will provide services to the appropriation teams, for example identifying customers and suppliers for them, raising awareness of their work and other supportive and administrative functions.

Applying organisational structures like the one described above brings the advantage of downsizing the projects, eliminates barriers to adoption and vastly increases the chances of success. Critically the cost of "Fail Fast Fail Often" is greatly reduced and shared within different teams giving the enterprise more chances to score a success.

Accelerated Transformation

It is not the strongest of the species that survives, nor the most intelligent, but the ones most responsive to change - Charles Darwin

In order to accelerate transformation in the enterprise, ultimately we are seeking to increase the adoption of applications among both internal and external customers. Adoption of applications that run on cost efficient platforms that satisfy customers' expectations within required SLAs is an important goal of digital transformation from an IT perspective.

A key step for IT departments is to determine which existing applications will be included in the transformation process, and it is precisely this decision that Accelerated Transformation seeks to inform.

In a nut shell, Accelerated Transformation is the process of determining which applications workloads should be prioritised for transformation. The criteria for prioritisation is balance between the cost benefit of transforming the application and the time it will take to complete the transformation, i.e. the time it takes to realise ROI. A simple way of thinking about the prioritisation is to think of it as the pursuit of high value, low hanging fruit.

The process of identifying applications and prioritising them must be industrial in nature to deal with the scale of the enterprise. What we mean by this is that we must be able to discern the key characteristics of the application (compute resource consumption, infrastructure dependencies, operating costs and potential savings from transformation) in a systematic and ideally highly automated fashion with only essential human interaction with the application owners, in order to minimise disruption to their normal operations.

There are three steps to Accelerated Transformation:

- Application Profiling
- Transformation Option Selection
- Application Pipeline Placement

Application Profiling

The purpose of this step is to gain enough information about the application to be able to choose a transformation option. The kind of information we require will be detailed and low level, for example including:

- The raw compute resource consumption (CPU, Memory, Disk I/O, Network I/O)
- Connectivity requirements (internal facing, external, etc.)
- Protocols used by the application.
- Integration with ancillary systems (use of SSO, Monitoring, Scheduling, etc.)
- The need for co-locality or specific hardware (for high performance or low latency applications)

This information will be gathered using automated means as much as is possible, but will ultimately require a meeting with the application owner and key technologists to verify the data, ideally by assisting the team to complete a standard questionnaire that feeds into application catalogue or database.

The information we gather will be used to judge our ability to migrate the application to a target platform either immediately or at some point in the future once any barriers to adoption have been removed.

Transformation Option Selection

Once we have profiled the application we can select the relevant transformation option. Each option comes with its own set of benefits and costs.

Option	Exclusion
Description	Application constraints prohibit transformation or the target platform cannot fulfil expected SLAs.
Benefit	This may be the most appropriate course of action for any given phase of Transformation, but remember everyone believes their application is exceptional and should be excluded.
Cost	It must be understood that applications running on legacy software and hardware will incur increasing costs over time.
Option	**Decommission**
Description	Applications considered too costly to maintain or which duplicate other functionality that is better implemented by other in-scope applications.
Benefit	Eliminating duplication reduces the overall costs of maintaining the application.
Cost	Any required functionality will need to be engineered in target superseding application.
Option	**Migration**
Description	Simple physical to virtual migration hosted on an IaaS provider (internal or external to the enterprise).
Benefit	Can be executed relatively quickly with minimal impact on application teams.
Cost	Offers the lowest ROI in comparison to other transformation options and may incur secondary transformation costs in future.
Option	**Transition**
Description	Application workload will be hosted on the target platform PaaS. For example an there may be DIY deployments of an application server in the enterprise that can quickly be transitioned to use the same application server hosted on the PaaS.
Benefit	Can be executed relatively quickly with minimal impact on application teams.
Cost	Will impact application teams as it requires some degree of technical re-engineering.
Option	**Transformation**
Description	Application will be re-engineered potentially to third party SaaS or otherwise to Cloud Native, Twelve Factor or Micro Service architecture.
Benefit	In the long run offers the greatest benefits in terms of cost reduction and customer experience through the utilization of commodity IT and market services.
Cost	Requires significant up-front investment and effort both from and technical and business perspective.

Application Pipeline Placement

As we begin to identify and prioritise applications for transformation, it is imperative to carefully plan when each application can execute on its selected transformation option. The reason is to ensure we avoid situations where we repetitively execute a sequence of tasks, exhausting all teams involved in the process and potentially causing disruption to the application owners when, in fact, we could have scheduled these tasks and executed them in one shot. Agreeing target migration dates and ensuring target platform capabilities are ready for on-boarding new applications is obviously vital.

Another key aspect of the pipeline is to report progress on transformation process. We shouldn't underestimate the impact of early success on long term projects and if we have chosen and prioritised our applications wisely, we should indeed find that we have Accelerated Transformation.

Community Software

Curiosity, Creativity, Collaboration and Contribution @sbadakhchani

The argument to the use of Free and Open Source Software (FOSS) over Proprietary Software is, hopefully, well understood and I have no wish to re-open the debate. Suffice to say FOSS is now well embedded in the enterprise, and IT decision makers have to operate in this reality.

Let's start by defining Community Software:

Community Software is General Availability (GA), FOSS software which is actively maintained by one or more commercial or non-profit entities that also offer professional services that appertain to the software

All Community Software is FOSS but not all FOSS is Community Software. Our definition has been chosen to help us decide between different types of FOSS when making an IT decision for the business.

When evaluating software for use in the enterprise, one of the key criteria is to ensure that we can sustainably support software liabilities in the most cost effective manner for the business. Remember, if you are not in the business of IT; every line of code, whether you wrote it yourself or not, is a liability.

For example, let's say you have a need for a job scheduler. You have managed to veto a proposal from an enthusiastic but misguide development team to write a job scheduler from scratch. You managed to explain to them that you are applying the NoDev principle, and that we are not in the business of creating job schedulers, we simply have an urgent requirement for one. If we are to do any development at all, we have to focus development resources on applications that will directly generate revenue for the business or improve customer experience.

You ask your technologist to find a freely available job scheduler and they duly return with some options. One of the options is a 'cool' scheduler that you can 'pull' off the 'hub' and start contributing code to right away, awesome. There are about 20 'developers' contributing code to the project, which is available as a Release Candidate, perfect, what could possibly go wrong?

The second option is an ancient scheduler that has been in General Availability for ten years. 'TimeCron' is also 'FOSSLY' available and you have a choice of a major software vendor to provide consultancy and support. There is also a specialist boutique consultancy that offers automation services that will ensure the scheduler will continue to work, without human intervention, even in the event of a missile strike that will destroy your primary data centre.

Given our definition for Community Software option one, the 'cool' scheduler is not community software. A loose collaboration of individuals that may or may not be actively developing the scheduler does not constitute a commercial or non-profit entity. This means you probably won't be able to purchase support services in any sustainable manner for the 'cool' scheduler.

The fact that the 'cool' scheduler is at release candidate stage also means it is not Community Software. The product isn't finished, it is incomplete.

'TimeCron' on the other hand has two commercial entities that can support it and has been GA for a decade. Furthermore if you had the need the budget you could employ the boutique service provider to implement a NoOps operations strategy. 'TimeCron' is clearly community software, and for the business Community Software is, in the majority of standard use cases, the right option as opposed to FOSS in general.

The above example may sound contrived but, believe it or not, it is real and all too common.

If you are to engage in development for a revenue creating project then using FOSS may well be an excellent option to kick start your application. Ultimately our principles lead us to choosing Community Software over FOSS for the business.

If one accepts the Free Software Foundation's claim that they are the representatives of the ethical software development, and the Open Source Initiative's emphasis on creating technically superior software then Community Software represents the buy-side, business interests of the software market.

About The Author

Hussein Badakhchani is a Distinguished Technologist with over 20 years of professional experience in financial services technology. Having worked for institutions such as the Bankers Automated Clearing System (BACS), Deutsche Bank and MasterCard Hussein has a proven track record of delivery in some of the most competitive capital markets. As a trusted academic, practitioner and adviser, Hussein also provides critical analysis of technology to executive and investment decision makers in Government, Banking, Financial, Commercial and Defence sectors. Hussein is also the author of NoDev, NoOps, NoIT Principles governing the ideology, methodology and praxeology of informed IT decision making.

LinkedIn: https://www.linkedin.com/in/husseinbadakhchani/

CIO WaterCooler: https://ciowatercooler.co.uk/members/hussein-badakhchani/

Cyber DB: http://cyberdb.co/about/

The Enterprisers Project: https://enterprisersproject.com/user/hussein-badakhchani

Twitter: @husseinb

The author wishes to acknowledge the following individuals for their valued contributions in the forging of the ideas expressed in this book:

Michael Duffy	Salim Badakhchani	Robert Lindh
Ben Van't Ende	Ehsan Noroozi	Jacques Le Bars
Junaid Mohammed	PJ Collins	Heather Murray

[1] The Electronics Handbook, Second Edition (The Electrical Engineering Handbook) 27 Apr 2005, Jerry C. Whitaker

[2] Prometheus and Atlas, Jason Reza Jorjani, London Arktos 2016

[3] I am aware of a case where a senior technologist was reprimanded for decreasing the number of manual steps in a provisioning process from 73 to 19 by automating 54 of the steps. These modern day luddites attempted to camouflage their incompetence with the subterfuge that "The technologist did not execute the task he was given, instead he automated the procedure" with no hint of irony. Suffice to say the capital division of this bank subsequently saw the attrition of their best talent to their competitor' glee

[4] IT Doesn't Matter, Nicholas G. Carr, Harvard Business Review 2003

[5] We have all, at some point in our lives, worked for managers whose sole function was self-preservation and we cannot deny that in some instances they have been incredibly successful, but at a severe cost to the rest of the business.

[6] One of the longest threads on the social media platform of an investment bank was in answer to the question "Are we a technology firm? I have been reliably informed that the thread is in rude health which is testament to the pathology affecting a large number of the IT department team.

[7] Back in the dot com days we used to say "You can slap my back as much as you like as long as you spank my monkey". This retort was used when flattery was used to as compensation as opposed financial remuneration.

[8] Ops, DevOps and PaaS (NoOps) at Netflix, Adrian Cockcroft, March 19th 2012

[9] Wise man say "If the people won't change, change the people". Duplication in IT is arguably one of the most embarrassing failures of Enterprise IT, and hence why we hear relatively little about it. It is equivalent of Zaphod Beeblebrox with one head (the new system) screaming for attention and adoption while the second head (the existing system) stoically enforces business as usual while sabotaging all attempts at change

[10] The worst self-service piece of IT I have had the misfortune to engage with was known as the 'project slayer' or 'das reaper'. It took so long to procure and install IT infrastructure using this 'service' (the worst case I was aware of was 18 months) that projects would simply miss their delivery targets and be cancelled or those initiating the project would move on. It was rumoured that the system was actually a means of controlling the IT budget

[11] Superstition in the pigeon, Burrhus Frederic Skinner, Indiana University Experimental Psychology

[12] Cooperation vs Collaboration, Monk West MonkWest.com

Made in the USA
Middletown, DE
18 July 2018